The *ORIGINAL* Book of …

Old Tyme Toys & Games

Kids Can Make
From Stuff
You Throw Away

Benjamin Jones
Editor and Publisher

Important
Creative Publishing Company and its owners are not responsible
for safe application of suggestions on building these toys and claim
no liability in their safe use and operation.

Printed in the United States of America.
Creative Publishing Company
11166 Frederick Pike
Vandalia, Ohio 45377 USA

Introduction

In every house there's countless stuff which are thrown away because they have served but one purpose. Thread spools and cotton reels may be taken as an instance. It does not occur to most people that these little wooden articles, strongly made and well-finished may, be put to good use when the thread has been wound from them. Yet from them quite useful stuff and nifty toys can easily be made. And so, it is with many other things—match boxes, broken clothes pins, cocoa tins, herb tins, eggshells, cigar boxes, nut shells, corks, old broom handles: there is no end to the list.

In the following pages we have set out to explain, largely to boys and girls, just how these odds and ends may be used for the construction of toys, games, and interesting models. The list is not by any means complete: such examples as are given are merely suggestive examples. The boy or girl who has patiently and thoughtfully made some of them will be able to devise and construct many more on similar lines.

Most boys and girls are familiar with those little *paper windmills*, which turn round gaily in the gentlest breeze—the ones which the rag-and-bone man gives in exchange for an old bottle. They make a capital toy for baby brothers and sisters, and they are very easy to make. All you need is a six-inch square of stiff paper—colored for preference—and two pieces of cardboard, each an inch square. First, you draw out your square as in Fig. 1, and then cut down the diagonals nearly to the center square. Now take hold of a corner and fold it over to the center. Secure it there with a small dab of glue. Serve each of the other corners in turn in similar fashion. Now glue on your two cardboard squares—one at the center of the back and the other in the front, covering the folded corners (Fig. 2). All you need now is a stout pin to push through the center of the cards into the end of a stick.

Fig. 1.

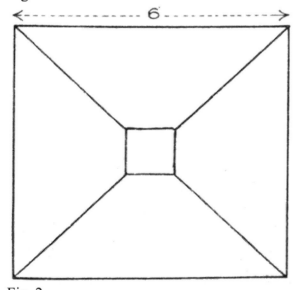

Fig. 2.

Now if you nail two strips of wood in the form of a cross, and pin on four or five differently colored wheels, you will have a jolly little toy for which baby will thank you (Fig. 3).

4

Fig. 3.

N.B.—We shall frequently mention the word "glue" during this little volume: therefore, we had better explain just what we mean. Unless we state otherwise, we refer to the prepared glue sold in tubes under various names and so on. These adhesives are admirable for all light work. They act best when put on thinly and allowed partially to dry before the parts are pressed together.

A very interesting little toy, which you can make in a few minutes, is the

Color Wheel. —Take a piece of white cardboard, and from it cut a circle about 3 inches across. Now from the middle of this cut another circle about 3/4 in. across. This can be done quite easily by putting a sharp-pointed knife blade into the compass in place of a pencil.

Divide the circle into seven equal parts, and paint or crayon the sections with the colors of the rainbow—red, orange, yellow, green, blue, indigo, violet.

5

When this is dry, make a large loop of string and put it through the round hole of the card; and hold the ends of the loop one in each hand. Now if you turn the string at one end as if you were turning a skipping rope, and then suddenly pull it tight, your card will revolve very rapidly, and you will find that instead of a colored card you have what appears to be a light grey one. This is really a little piece of science, for it shows that the white light about us is really made up of the different colors of the rainbow (Fig. 4).

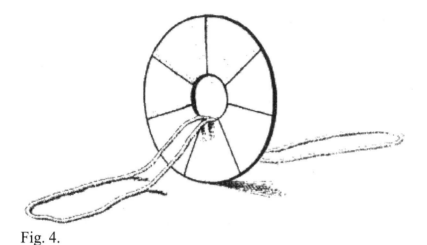

Fig. 4.

A simple Counting Top. —Take a piece of cardboard, and on it draw two hexagons having 1-inch sides. To draw a hexagon, first draw a circle with its radius equal to the length of the side of the hexagon. Then without altering the compass measure off the radius six times round the circumference and join the neighboring points. Now cut out each of these and from each one cut out one triangular section (Fig. 5). Scratch lightly along the other lines with the back of the knifepoint. Now bend these to form two five-sided pyramids. Close up the open space by binding the edges together with a strip of gummed paper (Fig. 6). When you have done this, place the two pyramids base to base, and secure them by means of small strips of gummed paper fixed along the edges. Bind all the edges in similar fashion for the sake of uniformity. All that is necessary now is to make a hole at the apex of each pyramid and push an ordinary safety match through (Fig. 7).

Now if you twirl the match in your fingers, and release it suddenly, the top will spin for quite a long time. To use it as a "counting top" or "dice top" paint the numbers 1 to 5 on the five triangular surfaces of the upper pyramid. Then when the top ceases spinning, the uppermost number is the one which counts.

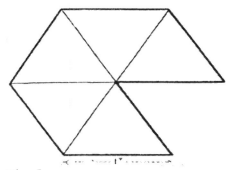

Fig. 5.

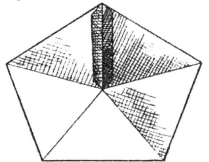

Fig. 6.

Fig. 7.

Tents for Toy Soldiers. —Boys who play with lead soldiers often find that, in making up a game, they require some tents for the camp. These are quite easily made either from paper or from calico. Their size will depend, of course, upon the size of the soldiers; and it will be quite easy to construct them to measure two or three times the measurements given here. Here is a picture of one (Fig. 8).

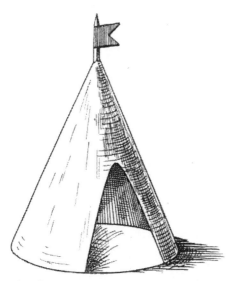

Fig. 8.

First cut out a cardboard circle for the base of the tents, say 2 in. radius. Now for the sloping canvas sides—the conical part, that is—draw out another circle, this time with a radius of 4 in. Only a part of this will be used; and to know just how much, roll the base circle round the circumference of the larger circle until it has completed one of its own revolutions (see Fig. 9). In cutting this out, one or two tongues should be left jutting out from the circumference: these fold over the edge of the base circle and secure the sloping sides in position. All we need now is a thin stick, about 4 in. long, to act as a center pole. This should be glued to the center of the base and should have the sloping sides glued around it. A little paper flag at the top will complete the little structure.

Fig. 9.

Most boys, and not a few girls, love to play at "soldiers" and there is no reason why each boy should not make himself a complete suit of armor, so that the game may be more real.

The Helmet. —With care this is not at all difficult to make: what difficulty there is lies in the adjustment and the size. First it is necessary to find out the distance round the head. This can be done with a piece of string; or, better still, with a linen inch-tape. Suppose the distance round is 21 in.: then the helmet can be made in seven sections, each 3 in. wide at the base. When these are brought together, they converge at the top to form a typical Norman headpiece (Fig. 10).

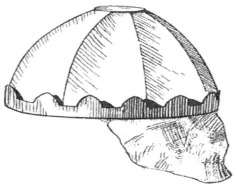

Fig. 10.

Using stiff paper, cut the seven sections as in Fig. 11. These should be glued together, so that the connecting flanges are inside. In doing this, it is very necessary to let the glue get nearly dry before pressing the pieces together: if it is quite fresh, the strain will pull the pieces apart.) Then at the apex of the sections glue on a circular piece of cardboard, about 1-1/2 in. across. For the ring at the base, cut a strip, just about 22 in. long, and having ornamented it in any fashion you please, glue the two ends together so as to form a circlet which will just go round the sections. Fix this to the seven sections with dabs of glue.

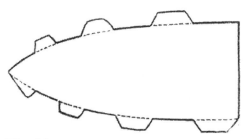

Fig. 11.

All that is necessary now is a coating of aluminum paint to give just that real dull metallic appearance. If this paint is not available, you can cover with silver paper, but this is not nearly as effective.

The Breastplate. —While there is less to do, and fewer sections to adjust, this presents quite as much difficulty as the helmet. It is best made in two sections. The exact shape can only be decided by trial: roughly, it is that shown in Fig. 12. The best method of procedure is to cut out two of these in newspaper, and fix them together with doll-pins, and then try them on in much the same way as a tailor fits a waist-coat—altering pins and cutting out shapes until the requisite fit is obtained. When this is done the two final sections can be cut out in cardboard (not omitting flanges), glued together, and painted. If you are good at painting, you can ornament the two sides with a heraldic device in crimson or gold.

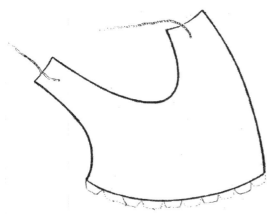

Fig. 12.

To fix it, when wearing, strings are used. Small holes are bored at the four ends (and eyelets fixed in, if you can do so) and knotted strings passed through. Tie the bottom pair across the back with a knot (not a "grannie"). Now take one of the ends of this and tie it with a string from one of the shoulder pieces. If the other shoulder piece be tied in similar fashion to the other back string, then the breastplate will be held correctly in position. The strings and all the back gear will be covered by the cloak and mantle, similar to that which knight in olden days wore over their armor.

Before you put the breastplate on you can tie a towel or apron to come just to the knees: this will take the place of the "surcoat" (and serve to hide your knickers).

For "greaves" or leg-armor you can cut out and paint cardboard shapes, like those shown in Fig. 13. These, when fixed with string, look quite well.

Fig. 13.

While we are talking of soldiers, we may as well give details of

A War Game. —Most boys are familiar with the game known as "Tiddley-winks," in which the object is to make small bone counters hop into a cup by pressing their edges with a large bone counter.

These materials can be used for a very interesting war game, consisting of the siege of a fort. The fort is simply a front elevation, like that shown in Fig. 14. This is drawn out in pencil on a piece of stout cardboard (or fret wood) and colored in with paints or crayons. The windows are then cut out; and the whole thing made to stand upright by the addition of two or three triangular supports (Fig. 15). These are hinged on to the back by means of strong tape or canvas, so that the whole thing can pack up flat.

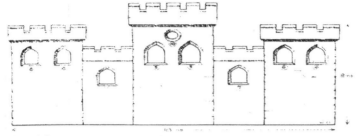

Fig. 14.

Each player in turn places his small counters (generally six) anywhere in front of the fortress. He is now the attacking party, and his object is to shoot his counters through the different windows. If he succeeds in sending a counter through a window, then he "kills" that number of the enemy. The winner may be either the person who secures the greatest number of "kills" in a certain number of attempts—twenty-four, for instance—or the person who first succeeds in scoring say 50 "kills." Any shot missing the fort entirely—*i.e.,* going right over or missing at the sides—is a wasted shot and counts one off the player's score.

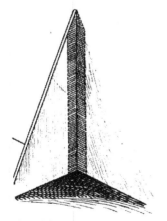

Fig. 15.

We propose to describe how to construct a simple *Toy Cannon*—
one quite easily made at a negligible cost and yet quite effective.
The only extra cost will be that of a piece of strong elastic: the
remainder being made of such things as cigar-or chocolate-box
wood. Fig. 16 shows the finished article; and a careful study of this
illustration will make clear much of the method of manufacture.

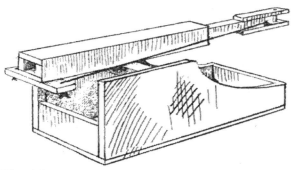

Fig. 16.

We commence with the stand. This is quite simple, being
composed of five pieces of cigar-box wood, a rectangular base,
two sides cut as shown, and two small end-pieces to give the sides
stability. The measurements you can decide for yourself: we
suggest a base 5 in. long and 2 in. wide, and side about 2-1/2 or 3
in. high, as being suitable to the thickness of cigar-box wood.

The cannon itself is not very difficult, if made square instead of
cylindrical. The barrel is composed of four pieces of thin wood
glued together as shown in Fig. 17. The pieces are about 6 in. long
and are cut and fitted to such a width as will leave a square hole in
which the rod can move easily. On the underside of this barrel are
fixed two pieces of wood - one about 1-1/2 in. long and 3/4 in.
wide at the end near the mouth: to this the elastic will be fixed. The
other, a piece about 1-1/4 in. long and square in section, is fixed
about midway along the barrel, and will act as an axle on which the
cannon can swing.

14

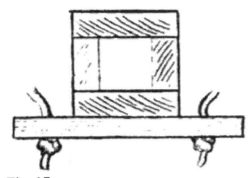

Fig. 17.

The rod by which the shot is ejected should be square in section, and about 5 in. long. At the rear end of it should be fixed two sidepieces to act as stops to prevent the elastic forcing the rod too far into the barrel. A nail driven through these two pieces will prevent the elastic slipping out each time the cannon is fired (Fig. 18).

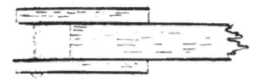

Fig. 18.

All that remains now is the fixing of the elastic. It should be slipped through the slot at the end of the rod, and the two ends fixed as shown in the first illustration.

If desired, this cannon can be used in connection with the skittles as described elsewhere, and in fact the pegs can be quite easily carved into the similitude of soldiers and used for the game.

Have you ever tried *Making Pictures with Matches?* —This is a very interesting occupation, and one which will fully test your ingenuity and your patience. Instead of using lines drawn with a

15

crayon to suggest a certain object, you replace these lines with match sticks, bent and straight, and so obtain nearly the same effect. You can start with the plain outline of some simple object such as a sailing boat or a truck or a house, and you can then proceed to more difficult shapes, learning how to suggest masses of shadow by placing match sticks closely together.

In actual practice, you get a large sheet of brown paper, and move the matches about until the right position is obtained: then you fix the matches to the paper one by one by means of a dab of glue. In time you will astonish everybody (yourself included) by the ease with which you can build up intricate pictures. Specimens accurately done and tastefully mounted make very acceptable little presents (Fig. 19).

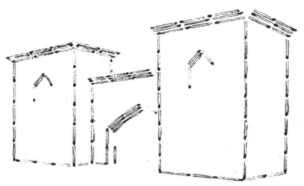

Fig. 19.

Deft fingers and a big fund of patience render it quite possible to construct

Models from Match Sticks, with the aid of just one or two accessories such as paper and glue. Placed side by side, and glued to each other, and to a cardboard or paper foundation, matches (particularly the larger sort) give quite an impression of solidity—which you will notice if you refer to the picture of the cupboard given in Fig. 20. In this a cardboard foundation is made according to Fig. 21, and the matches cut to the correct lengths and glued into position. In making the foundation, draw out carefully as shown, cut through the plain lines, and scratch along the dotted lines. Then bend into shape, and secure by means of strips of gummed tape or paper.

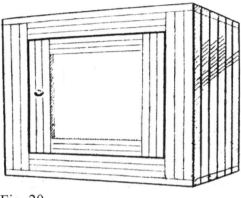

Fig. 20.

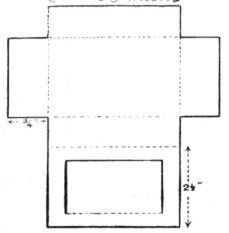

Fig. 21.

To suggest the panel in the door, glue matches round the outside edges as shown, and leave the cardboard showing in the center. If you want the door to open outwards, you will have to bevel the edges of the two matches where the cupboard bends, because, by the nature of the model, the hinge (that is, the cardboard itself) is on the inside.

In similar fashion you can make countless little objects—all varieties of dolls' furniture and fittings, money boxes, trinket cases, etc. If the matches are stained with bright colors, and tastefully arranged, and the whole varnished, some splendid effects can be obtained.

Talking thus of matches leads us to the description of another model in connection with the same articles.

This is a *Novel Match Striker.* —Any article which is useful makes a desirable present, especially if it has about it a certain amount of novelty. For instance, a match holder makes a nice little gift, and is generally appreciated.

If, however, it is of a type which the recipient has never seen, it will be doubly welcome.

One rather novel match holder and striker can be made in the following way. Obtain a funny picture—for preference, one that has a large figure in the foreground. Fig. 22 shows the type of picture we mean. Glue this on to a piece of stout cardboard. Suppose the picture shows a man's head.

Then let his beard act as the striker.

To secure this, cut out a piece of fine sandpaper, exactly the shape of the man's beard (or whatever it may be), and glue it into position on the picture. Then at the side glue on a little holder for the matches. This can be made of cardboard specially, or an ordinary matchbox cover can have the bottom stopped and be glued on.

As far as possible this should be a part of the picture.

Fig. 22.

All sorts of pictures can be done in this fashion: dogs, with strikers on the tail; pigs, with strikers on the back; elephants; grotesque men, etc.

If you like you can glue the picture on to fret wood and cut out the figure or a part of it, and arrange it, so that it will stand upright on a wooden base. This will tax your own ingenuity.

There is in every house one thing out of which the enterprising boy or girl can make any number of models and toys: that is the empty match box. Its shape and formation lend themselves to the construction of all sorts of things—houses, trams, dolls' furniture, etc.—the only other requisites being a sharp knife, a ruler, one or two pieces of cardboard (or better still, thin pine veneer), several large matches (or better still, match stales). These match "stales," which are particularly useful in toy-making, can be purchased from many hardware stores.

You can start with the simplest form of **Railway Truck**, consisting merely of the inner part, or tray of a match box, with two match-stick axles glued across the bottom, and four cardboard wheels secured in position by means of "doll pins" (Fig. 23); and then you can proceed to the most elaborate vehicles, bridges, buildings, furniture, machines, etc.

Fig. 23.

To give an idea of the method, we show how to put together a small overhead

Tram Car. —In the first place you want two pieces of veneer or cardboard, measuring 11-1/4 by 4-3/4 in. and 11-1/4 by 5 in.—to act respectively as the lower and upper decks. The actual method of construction can best be understood by a careful study of Fig. 24. The lower deck rests on four cardboard wheels. These are fixed by means of doll pins to two wooden axles (match stales) glued right across the underside of the lower deck. On this the structure is built up with match boxes.

Three covers are placed lengthways along each side and glued into position. Then above these come five match trays, which, when standing up, take up just the same space. These are glued into position, facing outwards, and projecting about 1/4 in. beyond the under covers.

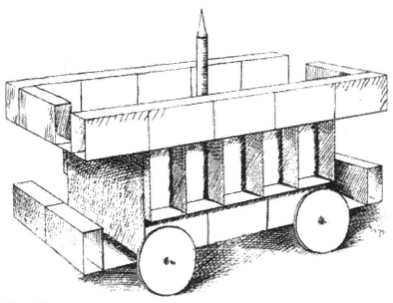

Fig. 24.

Across the top of the two sides so formed is glued the second sheet of veneer or cardboard, 11-1/4 by 5 in., to form the upper deck. Five covers placed end to end exactly make up a side for this, and one at each end completes the superstructure. Two covers, placed end to end, make a suitable back and front for the lower deck, while two pieces of veneer, 3-3/4 by 4-1/2 in., effectively close the inside of the car.

The trolley pole is provided by a wooden skewer, glued to the lower deck, and passing through a hole in the center of the upper. That completes the tram for all practical purposes. If you desire to make your model more elaborate, you can construct a cardboard or wooden stairway at each end, connecting the upper and lower decks; and you can replace the sheets of veneer at each end of the inside by properly constructed doorways; and so on.

Another excellent toy, constructed with match boxes—and one very much appreciated by little brothers and sisters—is the

Model Stores. —Once again this will be best understood by reference to the illustration (Fig. 25). The stores consist of a counter and a back fitment—the two mounted on a base board. For the counter, five complete match boxes should be glued side by side and then mounted on six empty covers. The trays of the five complete boxes should then be given handles to make them into drawers. For these handles nothing can beat a boot button. The small metal loop is pushed through a hole in the end of the tray, and then secured in position by means of a tiny wooden wedge pushed through the loop on the inside.

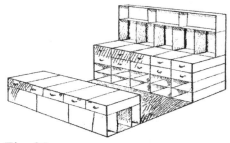

Fig. 25.

The back fitment consists of a block of twenty covers, five in a row, and four rows deep. These are glued into position. The two lower rows are deprived of their trays to make storage partitions, and the two uppers are fitted with handles as above. Surmounting this block is an upper fitment consisting of five trays glued together to stand upright at the back of the block, leaving a free shelf in front (as in most grocers' shops). Finally, there is a row of three trays placed endways on the top of the five just mentioned.

For "playing at shops" a little model like this is invaluable.

A Red-Cross Cart. —For this a large empty match tray is required. Across the underside a short length of match stale is glued, to act as an axle for the two wheels. These can be cut from either veneer or cardboard. A good plan is to cut out a circle in stiff cardboard and glue a covering of veneer on each side; this adds to the appearance of the wheel and makes it stiffer. If veneer alone is used, two circles must be cut out for each wheel, and glued together with the grain at right angles. The wheels should be fixed in position with doll pins.

For the tilt a piece of veneer bent over and glued to the inner sides of the match box will do quite well. The red cross may be painted on but will look considerably better if cut from some light red paper and stuck on. All that remains is to supply the shafts. For these two pieces of stale of the requisite length should be glued to the underside of the body of the cart. Fig. 26 shows the completed model.

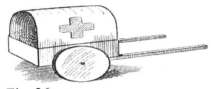

Fig. 26.

Another military model, slightly more difficult to adjust, is *A Maxim Gun.* —For these two wheels, each about 2-1/2 in. across, must be constructed in the manner described above.

The body of the machine is easier to make than describe. Fig. 27 shows the underside. A small match box is taken and along one long edge of the top a piece of stale is glued, projecting 1/4 in. at each end. This stale is the axle. Two full-length stales are then glued so that they meet at the end furthest from the axle. To render these projecting pieces more stable, a triangular piece of veneer is glued across them at the place of meeting.

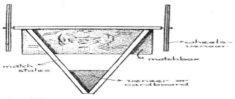

Fig. 27.

The two wheels are then fixed in position by means of doll pins. For the front of the machine a screen is required, and a piece of veneer or card is cut as shown in Fig. 28 and glued to the front edge of the match box. Through the hole in this screen will project the actual gun itself. For this a piece of wooden skewer or slender dowel will do. This can be attached to the top of the box by means of glue and can be wedged up into a horizontal position if found to slant too much.

Fig. 28.

A coat of dull grey paint will add greatly to the realistic appearance of this interesting little toy.

Many other things can be made, too, for use when playing with toy soldiers. One such model is

A Step Bridge, as shown in Fig. 29. This is a very little model, and one quite delightful to make. For it we require four 1-3/4 in. or 2-1/4 in. match boxes, a piece of cardboard or veneer, and some match stales.

Fig. 29.

The cardboard should be cut to the width of the match box that is, either 1-3/4 in. or 2-1/4 in., and to a length of 4-1/2 in. At each end of this should be glued the side of a match box. In this way the actual bridge itself is formed. The step is provided at each end by a match box, lying down, and glued to the standing box.

The remaining task is the cutting and fitting of the match stales to provide the railings—and this is the part requiring great care. Reference to the sketch will give a much better idea of the design than any amount of explanation. The stales will be cut to the following lengths: two at 4-1/2 in., eight at 2-1/2 in., and four at 2 in. You can finish off your model by pointing some of the stales; but this is not at all necessary if you have used a sharp knife and made clean cuts. If in fitting up the stales you find the glue is not sufficient, you can strengthen the important joints by use of doll pins

One other splendid use to which match boxes and stales can be put is the provision of the lighter sorts of furniture for the dolls' house. We give two examples typical of the extent to which these simple materials may be applied.

A Doll's Umbrella Stand is a very happy little idea—very simple but extremely effective. At the two ends of a small match-box tray, long stales are glued, projecting underneath to act as short legs to keep the tray from the ground. Near the top of these upright stales, four others are fixed to act as a strengthening frame. These last should be secured in place with doll pins in addition to the ordinary dab of tube glue. Then across the frame so made should be fixed one or two short lengths of stale to divide the stand into two or three compartments. Fig. 30 shows the completed stand.

A Doll's Fender is another article of similar type. For this we require a cardboard or veneer base and several stales. The base is cut out to measure at the most 5 in. in length; 5 in. by 1-1/4 in. is a very suitable size. Now on three sides this will have a rail,

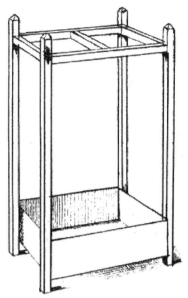

Fig. 30.

constructed with stales alone. A pillar is required about 1/8 in.
from each corner: this pillar should be about 3/4 in. high.
Stretching from pillar to pillar and glued to the base will be three
pieces—one a long one, approximately 4-1/2 in. long, and the
other two short ones, about 3/4 in. in length. Above these, and not
far below the tops of the pillars, will be fixed a parallel series of
long and short rails, fixed into position with doll pins and glue.
Very short pieces glued into an upright position between the two
long parallel rails add to the stability of the structure and improve
the appearance (Fig. 31). If you can stain the different pieces with
black and brown to represent iron and copper, then a very effective
representation of a fender will be obtained.

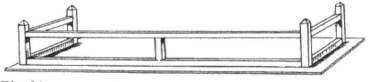

Fig. 31.

With a little ingenuity a set of fireirons—poker, tongs, and shovel—can be devised and constructed from match stales.

In similar fashion countless other objects can be copied in miniature with most pleasing results. We have not space here to detail the construction of anymore; but we would suggest that some of the following might be attempted: bedstead, table, chair, deck chair (folding), camp bed (folding).

The construction of one or two of these will doubtless suggest many more and reveal to the reader the boundless possibilities of this peculiarly fascinating pastime.

There is another broken household article on which the young toymaker may not cast eyes of scorn, and that is the broken clothes peg. In skillful hands, this is capable of reconstruction to very useful ends.

In the first place, if you can use a pocket-knife with some degree of skill, you will be able to chip out of a few broken pegs quite a respectable set of

Chess Men. —The pegs must be sawn across cleanly just through the center of the knob end: they will then stand upright. A few clean cuts with a pocket-knife will quite easily suggest a king or a castle or a bishop. The knight will, of course, provide most in the way of difficulty—as he is generally shown with a horse's head. A few painstaking attempts, however, should result in the obtaining of a credible likeness. Fig. 32 shows the construction of a "pawn."

Fig. 32.

Skittle Men. —Another piece of work for the pocket-knife expert is the provision of a set of funny skittle men for use in the game of catapult skittles (see below). These can be cut out to any quaint shape, and may be caricatures of well-known people, or of trades, &c. Much amusement can be got out of the cutting and painting of these little figures. Hats can be provided for them by gluing on little rings of cardboard (Fig. 33).

Fig. 33.

A Catapult Game. —Probably every boy knows what a catapult is—and what fun there is in the using of it. Happy young fingers pull back the powerful elastic, and bright eyes watch the stone go whizzing away. There is a fluttering of white wings: something falls; and there, lying in the road, is a motionless lump of flesh and feathers—all that remains of what was a beautiful little bird, pouring out its heart in joyful song.

Boys who think for a minute will not want to use the catapult in that cruel fashion: they will prefer a game in which no harm is done, in which no innocent creature is harmed, but which provides just as much fun. "Catapult skittles" is such a game.

It consists simply of a board with a catapult at one end, and a set of skittles at the other. The broken peg skittles dealt with above will do admirably for this (Fig. 34).

The catapult itself can also be made with two pegs. These should be cut off cleanly at the forks. Two holes, about 3 in. apart, should then be bored in the base board (for this, a piece of plank about 3 ft. or 4 ft. long will do quite well), and the pegs screwed on (see Fig. 39.)

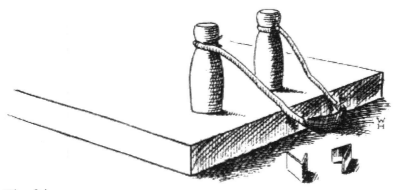

Fig. 34.

For ammunition all you need is an unlimited number of little pieces of cardboard, folded in two. These carry well, are quite heavy enough to upset the skittles, and, above all, are not likely to hurt, even if they do strike a player.

If you wish to vary the game slightly, you can rig up a "cokernut shy" in place of the skittles. This you will find very popular at Christmas time, particularly if you play for the nuts.

For this you want some wire hoops on which to stand the nuts. To make these, take a piece of stiff wire about 5 in. long and bend one end in the shape of a small circle, about 1/2 in. across. Now bend this loop so that it is at right angles to the wire; then when the wire is upright the circle will be horizontal (Fig. 35). Sharpen the other end with a file.

Make three or four like this, and then some more an inch shorter, and a third lot two inches shorter. These must then be driven into the other end of the catapult board so that they are not too close together; otherwise, the game is too easy.

Fig. 35.

Now all you need is a cardboard shelter. This can be oblong at the ends and triangular at the sides; but the shape is quite immaterial so long as the "shy" is properly shut in. Fig. 36 shows a suitable arrangement.

Fig. 36.

Another tip-top game, for the making of which you can use broken clothes pegs, is the "***ring-board***" or "***indoor quoits***." This consists simply of a board with several pegs projecting from it. The object of the game is to throw several rings in such a fashion that they will lodge on the pegs, scoring points according to the numbers marked at each peg. The board may be hung on the wall, or else placed flat on the floor. In the former case, the pegs must have a slightly upward slant, so that the rings will not tumble off easily; in the latter the rings must be upright.

To make either game, obtain a piece of wood about 18 in. square. You will probably need to join up boards for this. If you get three pieces of 6-in. board, each 18 in. long, and secure these side by side by means of a couple of battens, nailed right across the back, the result will be a square of the right size (Fig. 37).

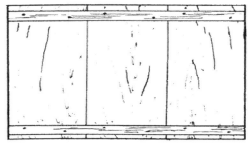

Fig. 37.

Now mark out the board as in Fig. 38. At the points where the dotted lines cross you will fix the projecting pegs.

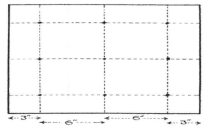

Fig. 38.

For these last take some broken pegs, and saw them off cleanly, just above the fork. If the board is to be a ground board, cut them quite level; if an upright board, then slightly slanting (Fig. 39). These must be secured in place by long thin screws driven in from the back—the correct holes having been bored in the base board. Now give each peg a number—assigning the higher numbers to the more difficult pegs—and paint the number on the back board close to the peg.

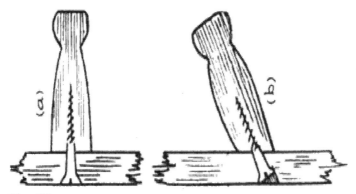

Fig. 39.

For rings various things can be used. Old brass curtain rings are suitable in some respects, especially for the ground game, but they are very noisy. Thick India-rubber rings are frequently used and can be purchased quite cheaply at any "games" shop. Rings made of stout cord, or thin rope, are frequently played with, especially on-board ship, where the ground game is very popular. Should there be any difficulty in obtaining or making any of these, then it is a very simple matter to cut rings from a sheet of thick cardboard.

The great objection to the upright game is the nuisance of the falling rings. This may be avoided partly by constructing a cardboard "catcher" to fit underneath. This is simply a cardboard triangle, or rather two right-angled triangles joined together by tape so as to bend easily and be strong: these are nailed to the two under edges of the board (Fig. 40).

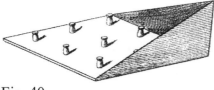

Fig. 40.

Another splendid shooting toy is the **Dart Box**. For this you need a wooden box of some sort. Size and shape do not matter very much, but a box with ends roughly square would do best: one 15 in. long, 6 in. wide, and 6 in. deep would be admirable for the purpose.

On the inside of one end paint a target, and number each division, assigning higher numbers to the spots more difficult to hit (Fig. 41). Now in the center of the opposite end bore a circular hole with a diameter of about 3/8 in.; and across this, on the outside of the box, fasten a strong piece of ribbon elastic—nailing down each end with a piece of wood (Fig. 42). For the dart, take a butcher's wooden skewer, and into the pointed end introduce a piece of a stout needle.

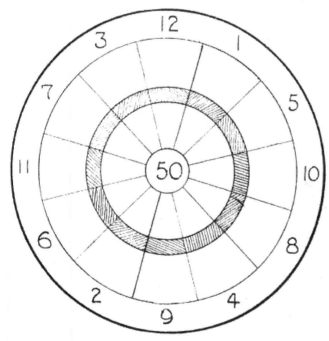

Fig. 41.

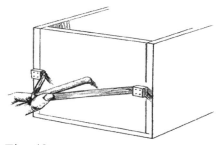

Fig. 42.

When shooting with this toy, hold the box firmly, open the lid, fit the dart in the hole from the inside, and draw back the elastic. When you have taken careful aim, close the lid and let go.

This is a capital toy and provides endless amusement. Also, it is a very desirable one as far as shooting is concerned, for the closing down of the lid ensures perfect safety.

While talking of making things from clothes pegs, we may as well give particulars of one or two things which will appeal rather more to our girl readers.

A Key Rack such as that shown in Fig. 43 is just such an article as a girl would take a delight in making, because of its simplicity and its prettiness.

Fig. 43.

The only materials required are two pegs, some hooks, and a length of ribbon. Take the two pegs—which should be nicely turned ones—and wedge the prongs one within the other so that the pegs remain fixed at right angles. In doing this, push the pegs in tightly, but take care not to split the pegs in so doing. Using a bradawl, make a hole through the junction of the prongs, and screw in a hook: the common sort as used on dressers, &c., will do quite well. Now bore holes midway between the junction and the knobs, and screw in two more hooks.

If now a coat of enamel be given to the pegs—say green in color—and if ribbons (pale blue) be tastily arranged as shown in the sketch, then a very pretty and useful little article will result.

Yet another splendid little article from pegs is a *Picture Postcard Stand*, for which the only necessities will be two pegs and a piece of wood for a base (Fig. 44).

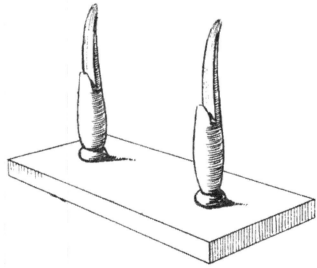

Fig. 44.

This base should be about 4-1/2 in. long and about 2-1/2 in. wide. It can be cut from wood of any thickness, but a piece about 3/8 in.

thick is the most suitable. Find the center of each end edge of the base and draw a line right across the wood. If now you measure in one inch from each end you will get the two spots to which to affix the pegs.

These last must first have one prong removed, or rather enough of a prong to leave a quarter-inch stump projecting. This stump should be rounded with a sharp knife, and then the whole peg should be finished off with glass-paper. These pegs must then be fixed knob downwards on to the base. Fig. 39 on page 34 shows a suitable method for this.

If you are at all skillful with your tools you will be able to cut a nice molding round the edge of the base, and so improve the artistic effect of your model.

Two thin coats of varnish, or of good enamel, will complete this attractive little article.

One little wooden toy, quite interesting, and very useful when playing with "soldiers," is *The Windlass.* —Some odd pieces of lath or cigar-box wood, a cotton reel, a length of string, some stout wire, and some glue and pins, provide all the necessaries. The cotton reel should be the largest obtainable.

Fig. 45 shows the completed work. First, make a square base for the windlass. If the reel is 3 in. long, cut off four lengths of lath (or four inch-strips of cigar-wood box) each 4 in. long, and glue these into a hollow square, two under and two over. Now cut off two more lengths, 3 in. long, for the upright supports—making the top ends pointed to hold the slanting covers.

Before these sidepieces are glued and pinned into position, it will be necessary to insert the reel. Get a piece of skewer, or lead pencil, 4 in. long, and glue it into the hole in the reel. At one end of

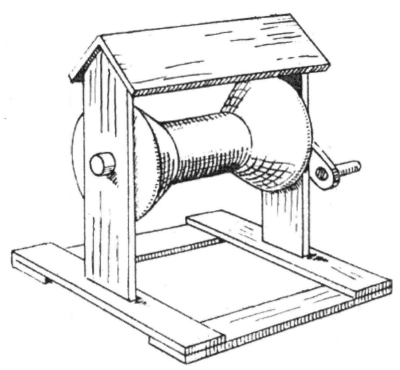

Fig. 45.

the axle so formed will be placed the handle. This can be made in several ways, either with wood or wire, or a mixture of the two (Figs. 46, 47, 48 on next page show some varieties, which may also be useful in making other toys). Holes just large enough to allow the axle to turn freely must then be cut in the side supports.

The two slanting covers should be about 4 in. long, to allow a trifle to project at each end and should be from 3/4 in. to 1 in. wide.

The two edges which meet to form the apex of the cover should be beveled off to form a clean join.

In making this model it would perhaps be as well to use carpenter's glue in place of the prepared stuff.

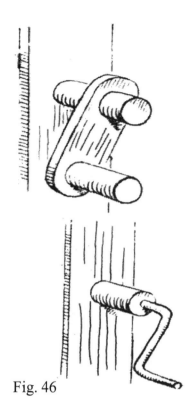

Fig. 46

Fig. 47.

Fig. 48.

From the material supplied by one or two empty cigar boxes, many interesting things can be made, especially articles for use with dolls—cradles, carts, furniture, &c. If these articles are of no use to you, they come in very handy for presents to little sisters and friends, especially when well-made and carefully finished.

A Doll's Cradle is perhaps one of the simplest to commence with. To a box from which the lid has been removed, it is only necessary to add two rockers. These can be cut out from the lid by means of a fret saw, and then smoothed down with glass-paper. Fig. 49 shows the best shape for the rockers, which should be glued on about an inch from each end of the box (Fig. 50). Great care should be taken that the two rockers are as nearly alike as possible, otherwise the cradle will not swing to and from freely.

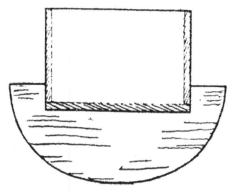

Fig. 49.

Fig. 50.

A Doll's Cart is also comparatively easy to make, the only really trying part being the cutting of the four wheels.

For the body of the cart use a cigar box which has been deprived of its lid and planed down level round the edges. To the underside of this body, and about one inch from each end, glue two pieces of wood to which to fix the wheels. Strengthen these joins by means of short pins driven through. Fix the wheels to these pieces by means of pins (Fig. 51). To support these two wheel-holders, stretch another piece across the space between them, at right angles to each, gluing it firmly to the two centers.

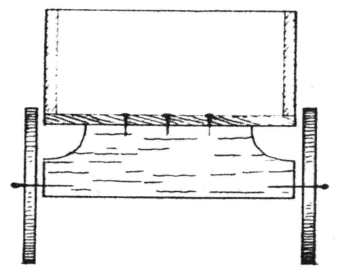

Fig. 51.

The wheels should be cut with a fret saw if you possess one. If you do not possess one, then draw out the circle on the wood, and cut the square containing the circle. Then saw off the corners to form an eight-sided figure and go on cutting off corners until you get down to the circle, which you can finish off with glass-paper (Fig. 52).

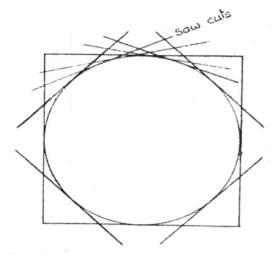

Fig. 52.

A little hook or ring should be attached at the bottom of one end, in order that a string may be tied on, and the vehicle drawn along.

A Jack-in-the-Box. —One of the most old-fashioned of toys, this never loses its interest. The box required for it is practically cubical: therefore 6 four-inch squares of cigar-box wood must be cut out. Two of these will need to be cut down to 3-3/4 in. in width, so that the four-inch bottom and lid will fit: so, from two squares cut a strip 1/4 in. wide. Glue and pin together the two 3-3/4 pieces and two of the four-inch pieces to form a hollow square. To this will be fixed one of the other four-inch pieces to form a bottom; and at the other end the remaining four-inch piece will be hinged (or wired on like the lid of a chocolate box).

Before the bottom is finally put on, it will be necessary to attach the mechanism. For this you will require a strong piece of spring about 6 in. long when released, and a doll's head. One end of the spring must be fixed to the center of the base. You can do this by means of tiny wire staples (bent pins with the heads nipped off) hammered over the wire into the base, and then bent back on the

41

opposite side of the wood (Fig. 53). At the other end of the spring a piece of cardboard must be fixed, and to it the doll's head must be firmly glued. When the mechanism is complete, nail on the bottom, and fix the lid.

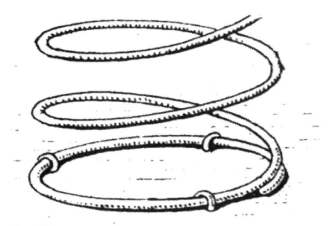

Fig. 53.

Into the center of the front edge of the lid drive a small nail, or stout pin, and on the box just below fix a revolving catch hook. This you can quite easily cut from an old piece of thick tin (Fig. 54). In this way an effective means is provided of releasing the lid and enabling the "Jack" to shoot out suddenly.

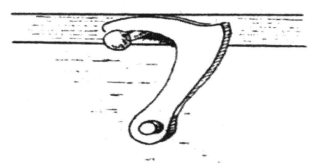

Fig. 54.

The Jig-saw Puzzle was at one time a very popular toy, and there are signs that its popularity is being revived. If it does not interest you particularly, it will provide a little brother or sister with endless amusement.

The puzzle consists merely of a picture (generally an interesting colored one) glued very firmly to a piece of fret wood or cigar-box wood. This is then by means of a fret saw cut into a great many pieces, shaped as quaintly and awkwardly as possible (see Fig. 55). These pieces are then jumbled up into disorder and passed on to the little one in order that the shapes may be fitted into place and the original picture reconstructed.

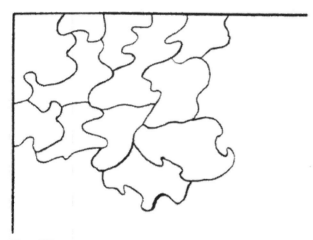

Fig. 55.

Somewhat after the style of the "jig-saw" puzzle just described is the

Geometrical Puzzle shown in Fig. 56. Each of these consists of a capital letter divided up by one or two straight lines into right-angled triangles and other geometrical shapes. While very simple to look at when completed, these little puzzles are by no means easy to solve when the odd pieces are given in a jumbled state.

The capital letters should be drawn on a piece of cigar-box wood, and then carefully cut out with a fret saw, or, better still, with a tenon saw if you have one. If you cannot manage wood, then the puzzle can be done in stout cardboard and cut out with a sharp thin knife.

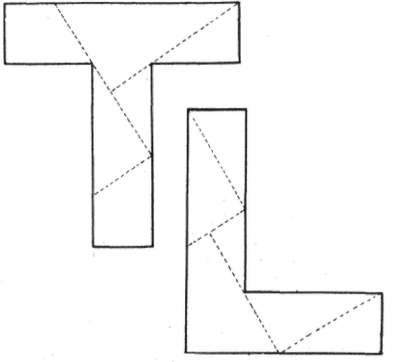

Fig. 56.

The Reels and String Puzzle is highly entertaining. The only materials required for it are the lid of a cigar box, two cotton reels, two beads, and a length of smooth string or thin silk cord. The making is simplicity itself. All you need do is cut the lid in halves and bore three holes in a line in one of the halves. Of course, you can ornament your wood as much as you like, but that will in no way increase or decrease the effectiveness of the puzzle.

When you have cut it out and finished it off nicely with glass-paper, thread the beads and reels as shown in Fig. 57. Take special care that you do not make any mistake in the arrangement, or your solution will result in a hopeless tangle.

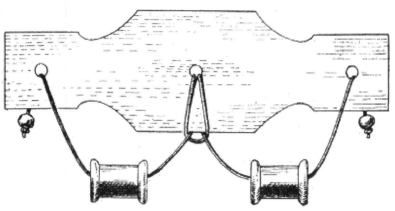

Fig. 57.

The object of the puzzle is to get the two cotton reels, which, as you see, are now on quite separate loops, on to one loop. To solve it proceed as follows: Take hold of the center loop and pull it down to its full extent. Now pass the right-hand reel through the loop. Taking care not to twist the cord, pass this loop through the hole on the right-hand side, over the bead, and then draw it back again.

Now if you follow the same procedure with the left-hand reel, you will find that the center loop is released and can be pulled through the center hole. Then will the two reels slide downside by side.

One thoroughly entertaining and, to a certain extent, bewildering puzzle is

The Three-hole Puzzle. —Really the puzzle consists of a piece of thin wood with three holes cut in it. These three holes are respectively circular, square, and triangular (Fig. 58). The problem is to cut one block of wood which will pass through each hole and at the same time fit the hole exactly.

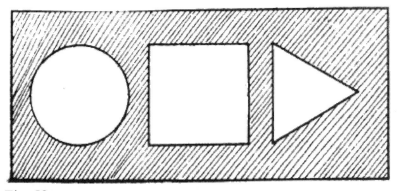

Fig. 58.

Can it be done? At first it looks to be quite impossible; but there is a very neat solution to the difficulty.

First cut out your holes. To do this get a cigar-box lid and draw out the three figures, taking care that the length of the side of the square and the length of the side of the triangle and the length of the diameter of the circle are equal. Now, using your fret saw, cut out these holes very neatly and precisely.

For the block you need a small cylinder of wood: an odd piece of broken broom handle will do admirably. This must be cut and finished with glass-paper so that it will fit the circular hole exactly.

Now saw a piece just as long as the cylinder is wide. This looked at in one way gives an exact square which will fit the second hole. Thus, two holes are catered for.

Finally, for the third hole the cylinder must be tapered on two sides. To do this draw a diameter at one end and then gradually pare away a flat surface till the triangular section is obtained.

46

Fig. 59 shows how the block, when turned in different ways, fits the three holes.

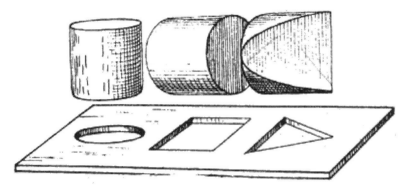

Fig. 59.

Another toy which can be made quite easily from cigar-box wood is *A Model Signal*.

First cut two strips of wood, half an inch wide and as long as you can get them, which will be 8 or 9 in.

These will stand upright on a base board and form the sides of the standard.

Now between these two you must glue shorter pieces of half-inch strip, to make the standard solid at the top and bottom, and leave a hollow slot, 1 in. long, in which the signal arm will fit and work up and down (Fig. 60).

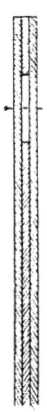

Fig. 60.

Now cut out and paint a signal arm, about 2-1/2 in. long.

Fix this by means of a pin passing through the two sides of the standard, and through the arm about 3/4 in. from the square end.

If it does not move easily in the slot, take off the top surface with glass-paper.

Before fixing the signal arm in position, bore a small hole 1/4 in. from the square end, and knot in a piece of twine or thin wire to act as a connection between the movable arm and the controlling lever (Fig. 61).

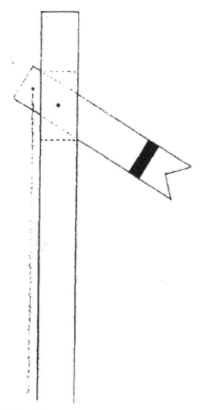

Fig. 61.

At the base of the standard fix the controlling lever. This consists of a small strip, with a pin passing through one end into the standard.

Adjust the length of the twine or wire, so that when the signal arm is down, the lever is horizontal; and when the lever is pressed down, the arm rises.

You can make a little contrivance for fixing the lever by erecting a small post close to the standard, and gluing on two stops, under which to rest the free end of the lever in its two positions (Fig. 62).

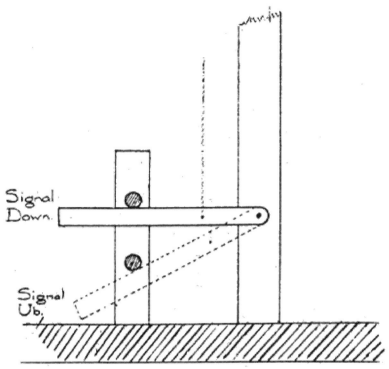

Signal Down.

Signal Up.

Fig. 62.

If you prefer it, you can have the controlling lever at a distance from the signal post.

You will then need a longer wire, and a little pulley wheel at the base of the standard. You must exercise your own ingenuity for this.

Another interesting little scientific toy, which has the additional advantage of being useful, is the **Weather House**, or the **Man and Woman Barometer**.

This consists of a little house with two doorways, at which appear two figures, one in fine weather, and the other in dull (Fig. 63).

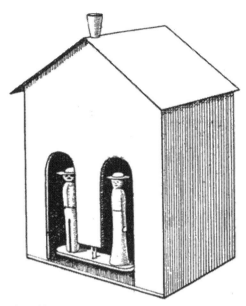

Fig. 63.

With patience and care this is not very difficult to make. For the house itself you can use an old cigar box, or, if you prefer it, you can make the entire house in cardboard. This is, of course, easier, but not very durable. If you are going to use the cigar box, you will need first to cut the lid and bottom into something like the shape of a house end. You will then have to nail the lid down and add two slanting pieces for the sides of the roof: and that will complete the house.

However, before you nail down the lid and put on the roof, you will need to understand the mechanism. First you will bore a round hole in the top of the roof, just behind the front gable. This hole is for a round peg to which the revolving base is attached.

The actual mechanism of the toy consists of a piece of catgut (an old fishing string, or a tennis-racket string). This passes through the center of a small flat piece of wood on which the two figures are balanced. Just in front of the string a piece of wire (a bent hairpin will do admirably) is fixed, to form a loop through which the catgut can pass (see Fig. 64). The other end of the catgut is fixed to the peg which fits in the hole in the roof.

Fig. 64.

For the man and woman, you can use two of the figures cut from clothes pegs. Screws passed through the revolving base will secure the figures firmly and at the same time add a little weight, and so improve the balance. When there is moisture in the air the catgut will twist. You must fit together the different parts and then, by turning the peg to right or left, adjust the position of the figures so that the lady appears in fine weather and the gentleman in wet.

A toy of unfailing attraction for boys—and girls as well—is *The Marble Board.*

This may be quite a simple affair—such as a boy can carry in his pocket for use in the playground—just a piece of wood, such as a cigar-box lid, with several holes cut along one edge, and a handle added (Fig. 65); or it may be a much more elaborate form intended for use as a table game.

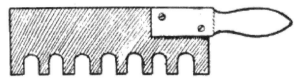

Fig. 65.

In this latter case there is a front board, like that in the simple form; but behind each hole there is a little compartment for the collection of the marbles (Fig. 66).

To make this you need two pieces of wood, about 2 in. wide, and as long as the table is broad: any sort of wood will do. These are for the front and back of the contrivance.

The front must next be marked out for the marble holes, allowing about 1 in. for the hole and 1 in. for the space between.

Of course, the wider the spaces between the more difficult it becomes to score.

These holes must then be cut out by means of a fret saw, or, if you do not possess one, by means of saw and chisel.

The back and front must then be secured in position by means of end-pieces nailed or screwed on. These should be about 3 in. long.

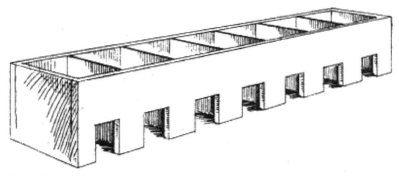

Fig. 66.

The next piece of work is the adjustment of the partitions. For these cigar-box wood is best.

You can either cut these partitions to the exact distance between the front and the back, and glue them into position; or else you can make them a little larger and fit them into grooves cut into the front and back: but that is a nice little piece of carpentry for you.

When you have done this, all that is necessary is to give the whole thing a coat of paint, and place numbers over the various holes—taking care that you do not put all the high numbers together.

Boards like this are used in the Colonies for a game known as "Bobs." Larger balls are used and propelled by means of a cue as in billiards. If you can obtain the balls, this is a delightful game, and one well worth making.

A Wooden Wind Wheel for the garden is a splendid little model to make—interesting in itself, but doubly desirable because so much can be done with it. Of course, it can be made quite small and very simple, and still provide unending amusement to smaller brothers and sisters; but for our own purpose it is just as well to make a larger and stronger specimen, one which can be employed as a power station for the working of smaller toys.

The main parts are: (1) a circular hub, about 2-1/2 to 3 in. in diameter, and 1 to 1-1/4 in. in thickness (for the smaller varieties a cotton reel will do admirably); (2) six or eight sails, each about 6 or 7 in. long and 3 in. wide at the extreme end, tapering down to a little more than the width of the hub at the other; (3) a hardwood axle; and (4) a driving wheel.

For this last a cotton reel will do splendidly, especially one of those with wide flanges and a slender center. The general arrangement is shown in Fig. 67.

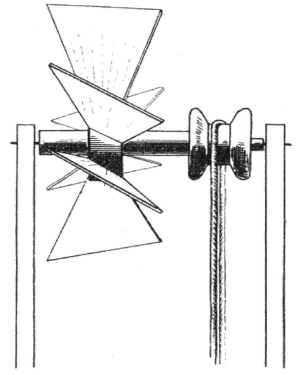

Fig. 67.

[pg 56] The cutting of the hub is not a very difficult matter if you have a fret saw. It should be cut across the grain if you can get a suitable piece of wood. The sails also are quite easy to make. For

these you cannot beat cigar-box wood. The cutting of the grooves in the hub for the insertion of the sails is the most trying piece of work. These grooves should be just large enough to allow the sails to fit tightly and should be cut at an angle of 45° across the hub. The sails should then be glued in with carpenter's glue.

For the axle secure a piece of round wood, such as an odd length of half-inch dowel-rod. This should be cut to a length of about 4-1/2 to 5 in. On this should be fixed the wheel itself, and, at a sufficient distance to prevent the sails catching the string, the bearing wheel. A French nail in each end of the axle will then secure it in position between the side supports and secure an easy running.

If you have a play shed in the garden, this apparatus can be erected at the top of a high post projecting through or at the side of the roof. The driving strings can then pass through a hole in the roof or the wall, and the power can be transmitted by a double pulley wheel and another driving string. If you have no play shed, it is not at all difficult to rig it up outside a window. You can try that and prove your own inventive abilities.

How to use the **Wind Power Machine***.* One thing which this mechanism will drive in good fashion is an overhead tramway system—a very pretty little toy when in working order.

For this all that is required is a number of cotton reels, a length of stout cord, and one or two of the model trams described on page 21. If you care to, you can make proper "standards" for the cotton reels. Fig. 68 shows such an arrangement. The flat base is for heavy weights when the system is rigged up on a table or other place where nails cannot be used. These reels must turn freely to allow the easy passage of the cable. In one place there must be a double reel (Fig. 69) for the transmission of the power. The lower reel will act as the ordinary cable wheel, while the other, glued firmly to it, will carry the driving belt from the wind machine described above.

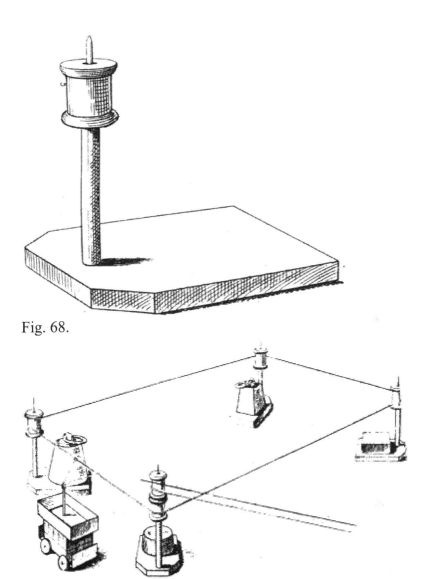

Fig. 68.

Fig. 69.

The model trams must be fixed to the cable. This is done by means of two wires, fixed to the pole of the tram, and twined round the cable. When this is connected up and the cable drawn tightly round the standard reels, the vehicles circulate rapidly on what is really a complete model tramway system.

Another interesting contrivance to which the wind power can be harnessed is *A Roundabout.*

This attractive little toy can be made quite readily from one or two reels, and four ordinary wooden skewers.

The first thing required is a base board, for which any tolerably smooth and heavy piece of wood will suffice.

Now in the center of this fix an upright piece of thick wire (a knitting needle will do); and glue on a cotton reel at the base of this.

In order to secure the absolutely smooth running of the roundabout it will be necessary to improvise some sort of "bearings."

For this there is nothing better than two hard glass beads.

If one of these beads be sunk into the top of the reel just mentioned, and the other fixed in the bottom of another loose reel, the upper one will revolve freely on the lower (Fig. 70). This loose reel will be the driving wheel of the contrivance and will hold the power band from the wind wheel.

Fixed to this running wheel, and immediately above, will be another reel for the actual merry-go-round. Into the sides of this uppermost reel bore four holes, and insert the pointed ends of the four skewers, arranging them so that all four are at right angles.

The running will be facilitated if another glass bead is sunk in the top of this reel.

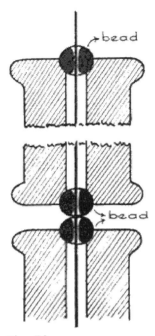

Fig. 70.

All that remains now to complete the roundabout is to fix four figures—horses, boats, or similar—at one end of each skewer.

These figures can be drawn on cardboard and cut out; or they can be sawn from fret wood.

Another interesting variation of this toy is the **Fairy Light Wheel.**

For this, instead of fixing figures at the ends of the skewers, obtain four eggshells, and suspend them by means of wires from the ends of the arms (Fig. 71).

Now if little night-lights or odd ends of candle be placed in the eggshells and lighted, a very pretty effect is obtained when the whole is made to revolve.

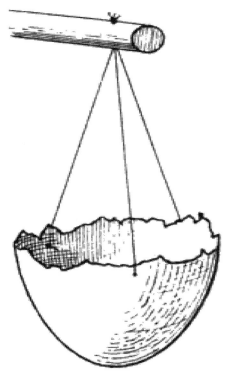

Fig. 71.

A toy which is always welcome to boys and girls is *A Pair of Scales.*

Moreover, this is a toy which can be made quite accurately with the aid of a few quite ordinary materials. To a pair of scales—or a balance, as it is sometimes called-- there are generally these parts: (1) a balancing arm, generally called the beam; (2) an upright standard on which the beam is supported; (3) two scale pins, and chains (or strings) to suspend them; (4) a base board to which the upright standard is fixed.

Fig. 72 shows the sort of thing we mean.

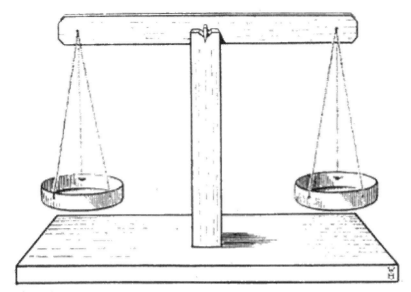

Fig. 72.

Now of these things not one presents any real difficulty. For the base board any piece of wood about a foot long, 5 in. wide, and 3/4 in. thick will do quite well. For the upright standard you require a piece of wood about 9 in. long and 1 in. square—one end of which must be fixed to the base board. The method of doing this will depend very largely on your degree of proficiency in the art of carpentry.

If you know how to make a mortise and tenon joint, that will be the most suitable. If you cannot attain to that, then perhaps you can make a hole just as large as the standard and sink the standard in the base. If you are not at all an expert, then you must just nail or screw your standard to the center of the base.

Before you do this, however, there is something to be done to the other end. You must cut a slot 1/2 in. wide and 1-1/2 in. deep (Fig. 73*a*); then you must cut away small triangular pieces from the centers of the tongues left (Fig. 73*b*); and finally, you must nail to the sides of the **V** so formed two little strips of tin (Fig. 73*c*).

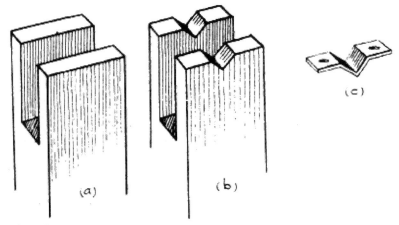

Fig. 73.

The next thing to be constructed is the "beam." For this you will need a piece of fret wood (or other thin wood) about 9 or 10 in. long and about 1 in. wide. To support this on the metal **V** pieces you will need a thin piece of steel—such as a piece of an old pocket-knife blade. This will be driven through the center of the beam and will project equally on either side (Fig. 74). Remember, it must fit tightly; so, when you cut the slot for it, do not make it too wide.

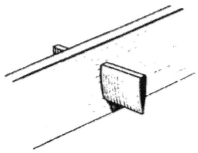

Fig. 74.

For the scale pans two canister lids will do quite well. Bore three holes in each of the rims—measuring off the distances with a compass, so that the holes are equally far apart, and suspend the pans by means of three strings passing into holes in the ends of the beam. If, when you have completed the work, the beam does not hang perfectly horizontal, then you must add weight or subtract weight from one side or the other. You can do this by paring off tiny pieces from the end of the beam, or you can stick on dabs of sealing wax till the correct balance is obtained.

If you cannot get any proper *weights*, then it is not a very difficult matter to make some. To do this, all that you need is to get some cardboard and a supply of sand, and to borrow a complete set of weights. First of all, make a number of little cardboard cubes, having sides varying from 3/4 in. to 3 in. Draw each one out on cardboard (Fig. 75); cut it out; and bind up with gummed tape—leaving one side ungummed. On one pan of the balance put this thing, and on the other pan put a proper weight (say 1/2 oz). Now pour in sand into the little cube until it exactly balances the correct weight. When it does, wet the binding, and stick down the remaining side. Finally print the correct weight on one face of the cube.

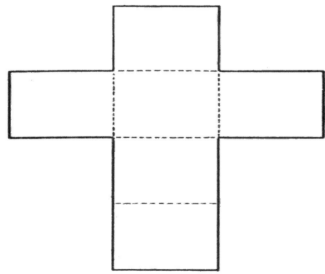

Fig. 75.

In similar fashion you can proceed to make all the different weights that you are likely to require, from 1/2 oz. upwards.

While not very substantial, these little weights will last quite a long time if they are handled with care.

Engines of all sorts are always fascinating to boys and girls, and later on we shall describe some excellent ones.

At this point we wish to describe what is possibly one of the simplest forms of engine known, and certainly one of the earliest.

It is the engine driven by a flanged wheel, which itself is made to turn by the weight of something falling on the flanges.

The commonest form of this wheel is the water wheel, where the weight of the water falling on the wheel causes the revolution.

As water is generally a "messy" thing to operate with, especially on such a contrivance as this, we have substituted something else.

For the working of very light toys, sand provides an alternative motive power.

If a flanged wheel be made after the fashion of a water wheel, and a steady stream of sand allowed to descend on to the flanges, then the wheel will rotate as long as the supply of sand lasts, and the power may be transmitted by pulley wheels for the working of some simple mechanism.

Fig. 76 shows *A Sand-power Engine.*
The large driving wheel consists of two circles of thick cardboard, each about 6 in. across, firmly glued together. These two circles are beveled, and fixed facing inwards, so that a groove is left in which the power band can run.

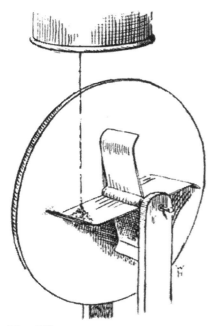

Fig. 76.

Through the center of the driving wheel thus fashioned a piece of dowelling or old lead pencil is fixed, projecting 1/4 in. on one side, and about 1-1/2 in. on the other. Nails are driven in the two ends of this axle, and the wheel is suspended between supports, glued, and screwed firmly to a base board.

The flanged sand wheel is next constructed. For this, four oblong pieces of cardboard, 1-1/4 in. wide and about 2 in. long, are cut out. A line is scratched along each of these about 1/2 in. from the end, and the cardboard bent so as to form a scoop to hold the sand for an instant. These four flanges are then glued to the axle, and the side of the driving wheel. If the sand wheel so made is not sufficiently firm, then another small cardboard circle can be glued to the flanges, on the side remote from the driving wheel: this will strengthen the wheel and in no way interfere with the running.

All that is necessary now is to erect some sort of sand supply: for this a large canister will do. A tiny hole must be punched in the bottom of the tin, and a revolving trap made with another piece of tin. This is simple enough: all you need to do is cut a piece of tin about 3/4 in. long and 1/2 in. wide and punch a hole in one end. This pierced tin should then be placed so that the unbroken end of the slip covers the supply hole. A forked rivet should then be passed through the hole in the slip and through the bottom of the canister and fixed in place (Fig. 77); the trap can then be made to revolve, and the sand supply started or stopped at will. The canister should be placed above the wheel so that a thin stream falls on the flanges and turns the wheel.

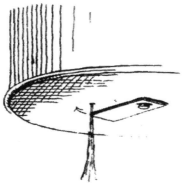

Fig. 77. If a string be now passed round the outside edge of the driving wheel, the mechanism can be harnessed to any toy and the motive power supplied. For instance, the contrivance can be erected on a flat hull similar to that shown in Fig. 83 and the power band, passing through a hole in the center of the hull, can be connected with the propeller by means of a rod (in place of the elastic). The resultant machine, though not highly efficient, is yet quite attractive.

Another material from which some delightful toys can be contrived is "tin," or, as it is more correctly called, "tinned iron." This is the stuff cocoa tins and mustard tins and many other articles are made of.

Perhaps the simplest toy we can commence with is

A Rotating Snake.

For this secure a clean flat piece of thin tin—the piece which the little patent cutter removes from the top of a round cigarette tin will do admirably—and, using a soft lead pencil, draw on it a spiral snake, such as is shown in Fig. 78.

Now cut along the lines with a stout pair of scissors, or else with a sharp-pointed knife.

Pull out the resultant spiral until it is stretched as in Fig. 79 and mount it by means of the tail on an upright piece of pointed stout wire.

The serpent will rotate on this for a considerable time.

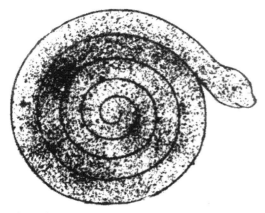

Fig. 78.

Fig. 79.

If you are good at bent-wire work, you will be able to make a wire
stand by which to fix it on a lamp chimney or gas globe: it will
then revolve continuously, and with considerable speed.

A Tin-can Steam Roller. —This is a nice piece of metal work,
and, when finished well, provides a proper little toy.

To construct it you need several tins—a round tin, such as a cocoa
tin, about 2 in. across and 4 in. long; an oblong tin, about 3-1/2 in.
by 3 in. by 2 in., such as the larger-sized mustard tins; a round
cigarette tin, about 2-1/2 in. across and 3-1/4 in. deep; two equal-
sized tin lids from canisters, each about 4 in. across; and a cotton
reel.

These, the main items, when put together, yield a model similar to
that shown in Fig. 80.

Fig. 80.

The fixing is quite a simple affair. With a pair of metal shears (or strong scissors) you cut away a portion of the top of the cocoa tin, to leave three tongues.

Then on the side of the oblong mustard tin you mark three lines to correspond with the three tongues and cut them through to form three slots into which the tongues may fit.

Now, if the tongues be bent outwards or inwards, then the two tins will hold firmly together, and give the boiler and cab of the machine (Fig. 81).

Before bending these, however, it is necessary to bore a hole in the underside of the boiler for the fixing of the front roller.

This is attached to the boiler by means of a narrow strip of tin bent twice at right angles and kept in place by means of a forked brass rivet or a strong brass paper fastener so that it will revolve freely.

This narrow strip of tin just fits over the cigarette tin—a piece of knitting needle being used as axle, passing through holes bored in the center of the bottom and lid of the tin, and through the ends of the slip.

For the larger rear wheels, the lids of two canisters can be used, or, if something is required giving a more definite impression of solidity, two flat boot-polish tins can be substituted.

Another piece of knitting needle passes through the center of these, and through holes in the sides of the cab, and so acts as axle. This is kept in place by means of dabs of sealing wax.

For the stack you can use a long thin cotton reel, or, better still, you can fix on another small tin by the method shown in Fig. 81.

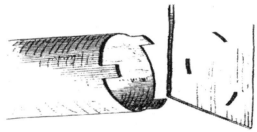

Fig. 81.

The turning of the front wheel can be regulated by means of two strings passing from the two right-angle strips through a hole into the cab.

If you can fix the strings to a piece of wood as shown in Fig. 82, you will be able to steer properly.

A hole in the bottom of the cab, and a piece of wood stretched tightly across the top, should enable you to set up the steering apparatus.

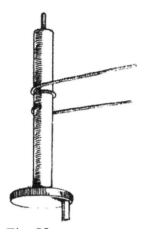

Fig. 82.

A Working Motor Boat.
To construct a motorboat that will travel a considerable distance is not really a difficult matter.

All that is necessary is a piece of board for a hull, a wood or metal propeller, and a yard or two of strong elastic: these, carefully adjusted, will do all that is necessary.

For the hull, a piece of 5/8 in. or 3/4 in. board, about 18 in. long will do. This can be cut to the boat shape by means of a pocketknife or a spokeshave and finished off with glass-paper.

It should be sharp pointed at the bows, about 3 in. to 4 in. at the center, tapering down to a width of 2 in. at the stern. In the center of the hull nail a block of wood, and to it glue two funnels (Fig. 83).

For these, the odd lengths cut off from bamboo curtain poles will do admirably; or, if these be not obtainable, a couple of incandescent-mantle cases will suffice.

71

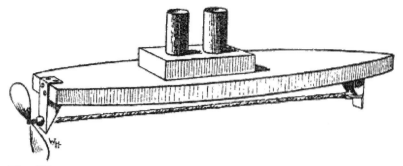

Fig. 83.

The adjustment of the motive power is the difficult task. First, you will need to purchase a couple of yards of suitable elastic: this is sold at most large toy shops, and costs usually a penny a yard. To fix this into place beneath the hull you will need to construct two metal supports. If you can get an old tin box made from metal sufficiently stout, that will do; if not, then you had better buy a piece of sheet brass, No. 20 gauge: 6 in. by 4 in. will be ample. Draw out these supports as shown in Figs. 84 and 85 and bend them into shape as in Figs. 86 and 87—one for the bow and one for the stern. Screw on the bow one about 1-1/2 in. or 2 in. from the point, and the stern one in the middle of the end.

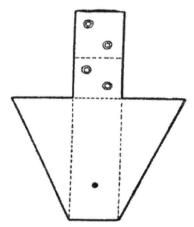

Fig. 84.

72

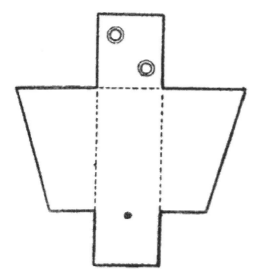

Fig. 85.

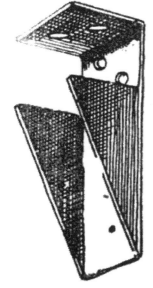

Fig. 86.

Fig. 87.

Now into the bow support fix a loop of stout wire to hold the rubber strands, making it sufficiently large to rest against the sides and so prevent turning. At the stern support adjust the propeller bearings. On the care with which these are adjusted depends largely on the success of the model. Take a piece of wire (1/16-inch brass is best) and bend it as in Fig. 88, introducing a hard smooth glass bead. This "bead" runs more freely against the metal, and so facilitates the working. Now stretch the elastic between the two loops, arranging it so that there are six or eight strands. To work the model, turn the propeller round and round till the strands of elastic are very tightly twisted, place on the surface of the water, and then release the propeller. Fig. 83 shows the completed model.

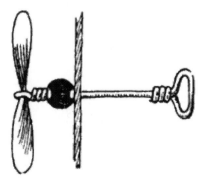

Fig. 88.

All boys love a toy that "goes"; such as a …

Steamboat that will actually travel on the water and will be very welcome. Our boat, which in reality is not a "steam" boat, inasmuch as no steam is generated, is very simple in its construction and possesses neither wheels nor pistons nor cranks, nor any of the things that one associates with a steamer.

The whole motive power is supplied by one or two candle ends, and a bent piece of strong metal tubing. This last can scarcely be called either "odds" or "ends"; and you will probably have to purchase it at a shop selling model-engine fittings, but a few pence will cover the cost. You must get an eight-inch piece of solid drawn copper or brass tubing, with an inside diameter of 1/8 in. (*N.B.*—Do not let the man sell you soldered tubing, for it will certainly crack when you bend it.)

The next operation is the most difficult: it is bending the tube to the shape shown in Fig. 89. This must be done very gently, otherwise you will crack or dent it. The loop shown should have a diameter of about 5/8 to 3/4 of an inch.

Fig. 89.

The actual boat itself can be of any shape. If you happen to have an old wooden hull suitable to the purpose, use that; if not, then a flat hull similar to that described on page 70 will do quite well. Fix the bent tubing at the stern of the boat, so that the two open ends project over the edge and dip beneath the surface of the water (Fig. 90). Two pieces of wire bent as in Fig. 90*a* will hold the tubing in place.

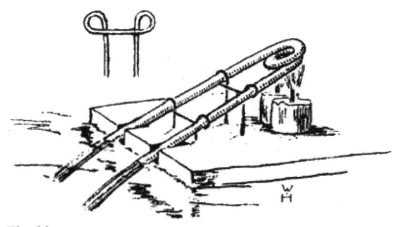

Fig. 90.

All that you need do now is place the candles under the loop of the tube and heat it. (If you have a tiny spirit lamp, that will act more effectively, of course.) The heat from the candles makes the air in the tube very hot.

This hot air is expelled from one arm of the tube: and a current of water rushes up one arm of the tube and down the other with considerable force. It is this current that causes the boat to move.

Another Working Steamboat This time our boat will merit its name—for we shall have a boiler and generate a supply of steam.

If you look at Fig. 91 you will get a good idea of the construction of this model and realize how simple it really is.

The boiler is provided by a medium-sized flat oblong tin, with the lid soldered down so that it is steam tight.

For the purpose of putting water into the boiler, when necessary, a hole is bored in the lid, and a cork fitted tightly.

Fig. 91.

In one end of the boiler, and towards the top, you must make a pin hole. When the water boils well, the steam is expelled through this tiny hole with considerable force; and to this is due the motion of the craft.

The remainder of the fitting up is soon done. A flat hull similar to a flat-bottom boat is prepared, and four flat-headed nails driven in, so that the four corners of the boiler can each stand on a nail head. The rudder is cut from an old piece of tin and pressed into a knife-cut made in the centre of the stern of the hull.

The boiler is placed into position with the steam hole facing the stern, and lighted candle ends are then placed underneath the boiler—as many as possible, for the more the candles the greater the heat, and consequently the greater the force of steam. It will help matters along considerably if the boiler is first filled with hot water, instead of cold; but be careful not to scald yourself in doing this. When steam is up, the boat should travel along at quite a comfortable pace.

Apart from the materials dealt with there are numerous little fragments. A pane of glass is broken, for instance, and in most cases all the pieces are thrown away. Now this is quite unnecessary, for from them can be made some

Japanese Wind Bells*.* Probably most boys and girls have heard or seen the jolly little "wind bells" which the Japanese people make, and which many English folk now hang in their houses. As they are made simply of slips of glass and pieces of wool or string, there is not much difficulty in their construction; and they are worth all the trouble you take, for their merry little tinkle is a pleasing sound.

The slips of glass—they are generally little rectangles, varying from 1 in. to 2 in. in width, and 2 in. to 4 in. in length—are suspended so that when a gentle breeze disturbs them the corners strike gently. To secure a proper suspension, you can either take a board, 6 in. square, and hang the strings from it, or you can make a conical wire frame, about 6 in. across, and hang the pieces of wool (or string) from the two rings (Fig. 92). The pieces of glass, which can be of any shape and size, should be fixed by means of sealing wax. It is usual to give the glass slips a few dabs of color, so as to give a brighter effect at night. If you can introduce one or two pieces of colored glass, the same effect will result.

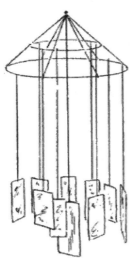

Fig. 92.

Other *broken* things, too, can be turned to account. One such toy, made up of things otherwise quite useless, is … *A Musical Box.* This entertaining musical toy, capable of producing the most beautiful sound effects, can quite easily be made with a few broken wine glasses.

So long as the bowl part of the glass is intact, it does not matter to what extent the stem or foot part has been damaged, provided there is enough of the stem remaining to insert in a wooden block.

The sound effects are produced by rubbing the ball of the finger gently round the rim of the glass. For this the fingertip must be absolutely clean, particularly of any grease, and must be thoroughly wet.

Probably for the first time or two of rubbing nothing will occur.

If that is so, continue wetting the finger, and rub it on an India-rubber sponge or a piece of soft India-rubber. You will know at once when the fingertip is in the right condition, for it will commence to "drag" on the rim.

Eventually a most beautiful pealing note will be emitted, which note will alter slightly in tone if water be poured into the glass.

If in this way you can secure eight glasses tuned exactly to an octave, then you have the wherewithal to produce tunes.

When you have obtained the glasses, then it is quite easy to fit them into a box quite close together, leaving just enough room for the fingers to move round.

Blocks of wood must be nailed to the bottom of the box, and holes bored in these blocks just exactly large enough to admit the stem (see Fig. 93).

Fig. 93.

A Fleet of Nutshell Boats floating on a bowl of water creates a very pretty little picture—nor are these little crafts at all difficult to make.

For the hull a nice evenly shaped walnut shell is required: this should be cleaned out, trimmed with a sharp knife (be CAREFUL), and scrubbed with a stiff brush.

For the mast a matchstick will suffice.

To keep this in position glue two match sticks right across the widest part of the hull—one on each side of the mast—and then put a daub of glue at the bottom of the hull and others where the crossbars touch the mast.

The sail consists merely of a piece of paper with two holes through which the mast passes.

A glance at Fig. 94 will reveal the method of fitting up and show what a trim little craft can result from such a simple origin.

Fig. 94.

One other toy which has always been deservedly popular is
The Jumping Frog. If you are skillful with your pocketknife you
can cut out a representation of the animal from a lump of wood,
and paint it to make it more realistic. If, however, you have not the
requisite skill, you can still construct the toy by using a walnut
shell in place of the carved model. In either case the actual
mechanism for "jumping" is the same.

You want a good-sized shell, or rather half-shell, some very strong
thin twine, and a match. First you must bore two holes in the sides
of the shell, not too near the edge, then tie a loop of twine round
the holes and the edge (Fig. 95). Now if you put a piece of
matchstick between the strings, and twist the string by turning the
match round, you will complete the jumping mechanism (Fig. 96).
Keep your finger on the match to prevent it flying back, and
carefully turn the shell upside down on the table, holding it all the

time. Now if you press one finger on the side of the shell so that it slips suddenly from under, then your frog will perform an astounding leap in the air. But, in your eagerness to get a big jump, do not twist the string too tightly, otherwise the holes will break out.

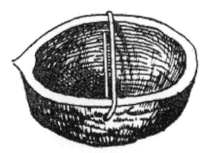

Fig. 95.

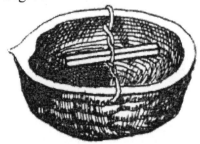

Fig. 96.

If, as mentioned earlier, you are skillful enough to cut out the frog, you will need to hollow out the body so that there will be room for the turning of the match.

You can also do very much the same with a fowl's "wishbone" if you tie a loop of string round the two prongs and use the match as shown above.

The shell of an ordinary hen's egg does not seem to give much scope for construction. Yet much can be done with it.

One of the best things you can make is

An Egg-shell Yacht. Next time mother is making cakes, or anything which needs eggs, tell her you want the shell intact, and ask her to let you blow out the contents. To do this, bore a small hole at each end, and blow. Of course, if you have ever collected birds' eggs, and are an adept at egg-blowing, you will only need one hole.

Stop up the holes with sealing wax or plasticene. This complete shell is to form the hull of the yacht; it will be necessary to add a keel, mainmast, bowsprit, &c., to finish the craft.

For the mainmast get a very thin piece of wood—a very thin piece of bamboo or a piece of split cane will do—and pass it carefully through two holes which have previously been bored in the opposite sides of the shell. Let it project an inch or two below (Fig. 97*a*). Fix in position by means of sealing wax. In similar fashion arrange a bowsprit.

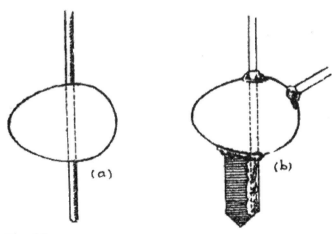

Fig. 97.

As the hull is very light, it will be necessary to have a good steadying keel. A piece of sheet lead about 2 in. long and 1 in.

83

wide will do admirably. Secure it to the shell and the projecting piece of mainmast by means of sealing wax (Fig. 97b).

Now if this floats properly you can proceed with the rigging, which may be as simple or as elaborate as you please. Fasten the spars to the mainmast by means of very thin wire. (Sealing wax will do but is not at all reliable for this.) For the sails use tough tissue paper, gluing the main and top sails in position, and fixing the jib and foresails by means of threads.

The addition of a cardboard rudder—fixed by wax—will complete a trim little craft which will sail in approved regatta fashion, if it has been properly adjusted (Fig. 98).

Fig. 98.

Nor must broke eggshells be despised. These can be decorated with paints, and some very amusing little articles provided. Legs and arms can be added, fixed into place with dabs of sealing wax; clothes can be devised; and grotesque little toys improvised—toys suitable for the decoration of the Christmas tree or sale at bazaars.

Quite a number of amusing little toys can be made from those cylindrical cardboard cases in which incandescent mantles are usually sold. For the most part the only things needed for the construction are a sharp knife (one with a very thin blade preferred), a tube of glue, one or two odd pieces of cardboard, and some paints.

A Money Box, for instance, is always useful, and, by the aid of the paint box, can be made very attractive.

Take off the two end covers, and glue one end of the case to a circle of thick cardboard, about 1/4 in. larger in radius than the case. Now for the other end construct a conical top. To do this, draw out a circle with a radius of about 1-1/4 in. and cut out a sector. The two ends can then be brought together and fixed with a piece of glued tape, and the whole thing can be glued to the other end of the case.

Before this is done, however, the money slot should be cut in the side. Much can be done to make the article attractive by a judicious use of the paints. The money slot, for instance, can be regarded as the mouth, and a grotesque face drawn round it.

If you care to cover the conical top with felt or flannel, you can make the model very funny indeed. In the spring you can damp the felt or flannel and spread on grass seeds: these will grow and give your grotesque figure a fine crop of bright green hair (Fig. 99). Of course, if you are going to damp the upper parts of the model, you must obtain and use some sort of waterproof glue.

Fig. 99.

A Pin-hole Camera is another extremely simple yet extraordinarily interesting contrivance (Fig. 100).

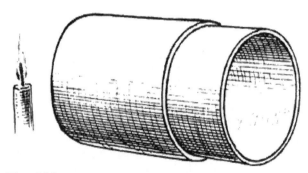

Fig. 100.

For this you require two mantle cases, one just large enough to slide easily into the other. Take the smaller one and cover one end with tissue paper.

This must be done neatly and strongly, otherwise, as the case slides up and down in the outer one, the tissue will tear. You should draw out on the tissue a circle just as large as the end of the case, and then all round, draw and cut little pointed tags to lap over the edges and stick down (Fig. 101).

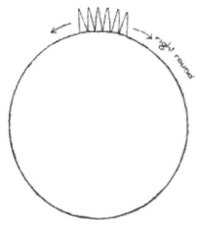

Fig. 101.

One end of the outer case should be covered with thick brown paper in just the same way, and a tiny pin hole pricked exactly in the centre of the brown-paper end.

Now if a lighted candle be placed near to the pin hole, and if the inner case be moved to and from until the right spot is found, an exact picture of the candle flame will be seen on the tissue paper.

A Doll's Easy Chair.
Apart from accurate and careful cutting there is not very much difficulty in this. Take a mantle case and remove the covers. Now draw a line from end to end and use this as a base line, measuring the distances to right and left to the different points: this will ensure accuracy.

Fig. 102 shows one design suitable for the purpose; but you would possibly like to make up your own. The fitting of the seat is done as follows: On a piece of cardboard mark out a circle having the same radius as the case, and another circle with a radius 1/8 in.

larger. Cut this out as shown in Fig. 103. Now cut a slot a little more than half-way across the case from the front, at a level suitable for the seat, and into this slide the seat. If the slot has not been cut far enough across, go on cutting till the seat fits correctly in the case. Then glue it in position.

Fig. 102.

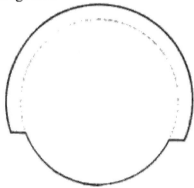

Fig. 103.

All that is now required is a coat of paint, and any ornamentation you may care to add.

In conclusion we would point out once more what we stated at the beginning—namely, that the examples given are intended merely to suggest ways and means of making countless other articles.

Creative Publishing Co

Made in the USA
Columbia, SC
27 January 2023

10619003R00050